HAL LEONARD
GUITAR METHOD
Supplement to Any Guitar Method

FINGERPICKING GUITAR

DOUG BODUCH

T0210351

CONTENTS

To access audio and video visit:
www.halleonard.com/mylibrary

Enter Code
6101-3627-4112-1531

ISBN 978-1-70511-358-5

A Muse Group Company

Visit Hal Leonard Online at
www.halleonard.com

World headquarters, contact:
Hal Leonard
7777 West Bluemound Road
Milwaukee, WI 53213
Email: info@halleonard.com

In Europe, contact:
Hal Leonard Europe Limited
Dettingen Way
Bury St Edmunds, Suffolk, IP33 3YB
Email: info@halleonardeurope.com

In Australia, contact:
Hal Leonard Australia Pty. Ltd.
4 Lentara Court
Cheltenham, Victoria, 3192 Australia
Email: info@halleonard.com.au

INTRODUCTION

Welcome to the *Hal Leonard Fingerpicking Guitar Method*. This book supplements the concepts and techniques taught in the basic *Hal Leonard Guitar Method*, but it focuses on using the right-hand fingers (rather than a pick) to pluck the strings. We'll start off learning proper right-hand technique, playing some melodies and accompaniment and working our way to playing some fingerpicking solo arrangements. You can use any type of guitar: acoustic, electric, or nylon-string. The exercises and songs will be written in both standard notation and tablature (tab), and they will also have an accompanying video ▣ or audio ◑ example online. To view these videos or listen to the audio, go to *www.halleonard.com/mylibrary* and enter the code found on page 1 (title page). You can either stream the examples or download them all to your computer.

RIGHT HAND CONCEPTS

Since we'll be using our right-hand fingers to pluck the strings, it will be helpful to identify each finger. The fingers of the right hand will be labeled by the following letters:

p = thumb

i = index finger

m = middle finger

a = ring finger

These letters/abbreviations come from the Spanish names for the fingers, and they are used in classical guitar notation. It's helpful to label these differently than the left-hand fingers to avoid confusion. Typically, the pinky is not used for fingerpicking, except for some flamenco techniques. In that case, it is labeled as *c* or *e*.

This book is written from a right-hand perspective, in which the right hand plucks and the left hand frets. If you are a left-handed player, simply reverse the directions.

In general, keep the right-hand fingers and wrist arched, as in the picture.

Notice that you should keep some space between the wrist and the top of the guitar. This allows the fingers to more efficiently pluck the strings. The right-hand thumb should also be outside of the fingers, as in the picture.

When plucking with the fingers, avoid lifting the hand, but rather, let each finger do the work, moving mainly from the first knuckle joint. In general, the thumb will play the lowest three strings with downstrokes, while the fingers will play the higher three strings with upstrokes. There will be times when the thumb plays the higher strings or the fingers will play lower, but more often than not, the first rule will apply.

PLAYING WITH THE FINGERS

Another general rule of fingerpicking is that the index/first finger (*i*) will pluck the third string, the middle/second finger (*m*) will pluck the second string, and the ring/third finger (*a*) will pluck the first string. Let's try that in the following example, using some open strings.

To access this video and others, go to *www.halleonard.com/mylibrary* and input the code found on page 1!

Ex. 1

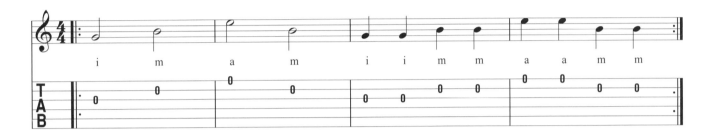

Keeping those same concepts in mind, let's play a popular melody.

Ex. 2

HAPPY BIRTHDAY TO YOU

Words and Music by Mildred J. Hill and Patty S. Hill

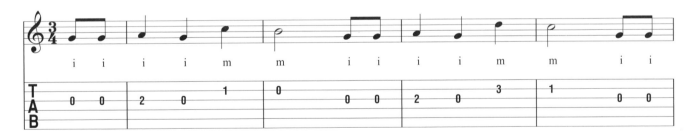

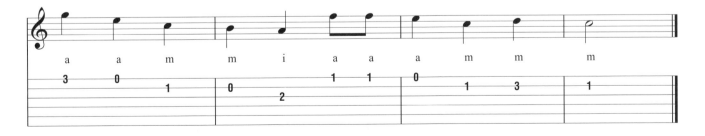

Now that you are used to playing each string with a specific finger, it's time to break the rules. While the string/finger relationship works well for arpeggios and accompaniment patterns, it's not always the best choice for playing melodies. In fact, we can approach fingerpicking with one of the same concepts we use for playing with a pick: alternating. Since playing with one finger repeatedly isn't the most efficient method, we can alternate fingers much like when we use downstrokes and upstrokes with the pick. The most common fingers to alternate are *i* and *m*. You can start with either finger. Sometimes, one finger will be an obvious better choice, as it will lead to easier string crossings. Because of the way the fingers of the hand are positioned, it's easier to go to a higher string with the *m* finger and easier to come down to a lower string with the *i* finger. But rarely does a piece work out where it's always an easy crossing, so we need to get comfortable with those "uncomfortable" string crossings.

Let's try "Happy Birthday" again, this time using alternating fingers. Start with *i* the first time, then repeat it starting with *m*.

Ex. 3

HAPPY BIRTHDAY TO YOU

Words and Music by Mildred J. Hill and Patty S. Hill

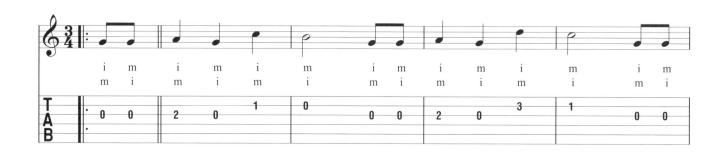

If you felt more comfortable repeating a finger instead of alternating, that is completely normal. It takes time to get used to playing with the fingers, and there is definitely a more secure feeling created by limiting one finger per string. In the next few melodies, play whatever feels most comfortable, with the eventual goal of getting used to alternating fingers. Notice in the video that we can rest our right-hand thumb lightly on the sixth string to add some stability while the fingers pluck the strings.

ALTERNATING OTHER FINGERS

You may be wondering about using other fingers to alternate, such as *m–a* or *i–a*. Those options do exist, but generally, it's easiest and most comfortable to stick with *i–m*. But rest assured, there will be times when the other fingers need to alternate. In the end, it's always up to you what fingers you want to use. There may be suggested fingerings, but there is no right or wrong.

For the next two songs, try alternating *i* and *m* to play the melody. Of course, you can use a single finger to play each song, but if you challenge yourself here, then you'll be able to take on even greater heights later!

Ex. 4

JINGLE BELLS

Words and Music by J. Pierpont

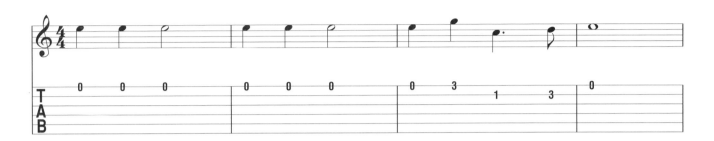

ODE TO JOY

By Ludwig van Beethoven

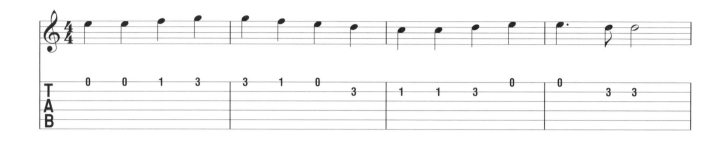

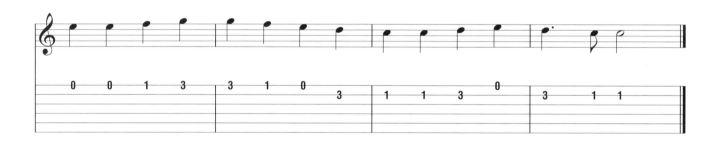

USING THE THUMB

Now that you are hopefully feeling comfortable with the fingers, let's try playing some notes using the thumb. As stated before, the thumb will generally take care of playing the lower strings 4, 5, and 6. Occasionally, we'll play higher strings with the thumb, but for now, this will be a fine rule to follow. We'll play downstrokes with the thumb, plucking notes on the side of the thumb farthest from the fingers. When playing with the thumb, we can keep our fingers resting gently on the top three strings, or just hovering over them in a relaxed state. Hold your wrist and arm in a manner that allows the thumb to play and follow through without bumping the fingers. We don't want the thumb getting caught underneath the fingers.

First, let's just play some open notes with the thumb.

Ex. 6

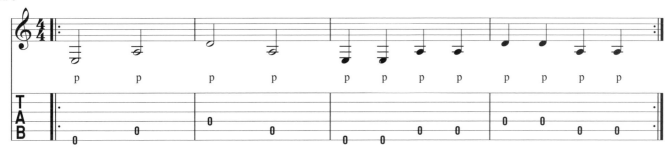

Now we'll play some popular melodies using only the thumb. Note that when playing just with the thumb, we can rest our fingers on the highest three strings, adding stability to the hand. (This is similar to what we did when we played with the fingers and rested our thumb on the lowest string.) These small points of contact can be helpful in creating a home base for the hand. You'll often see players resting the pad of their hand lightly on the bridge or even having the pinky lightly touch the soundboard. If you do employ any of these techniques, just be sure they are not rigidly fixed and creating any tension. The goal is to have a relaxed and stable, tension-free right hand.

REDEMPTION SONG

Words and Music by Bob Marley

Ex. 7

DAY TRIPPER

Words and Music by John Lennon and Paul McCartney

Ex. 8

Play 4 times

PLAYING TWO NOTES AT ONCE

We'll look at two ways to play notes together: using two different fingers or with fingers and thumb. The important goal here is to be able to pluck both strings at the same time. When starting out, it will be helpful to *plant* the fingers on the strings before plucking them. This planting technique will create a rest, but eventually, you'll be able to keep those fingers lined up and pluck without placing them on the strings first. For now, let's try an exercise with the planting technique. Use *i–m* to pluck the strings on beats 1 and 3, then bring your fingers to rest on the strings on beats 2 and 4. (We've also included fingerings for your left hand—"0" = open, "1" = index, and so on.)

Ex. 9

For the next exercise, continue with the planting technique but with a less pronounced effect. In other words, the goal is for that rest to disappear. Again, use *i–m* throughout.

Ex. 10

We can also play a similar exercise on the first two strings, this time using *m–a.*

Ex. 11

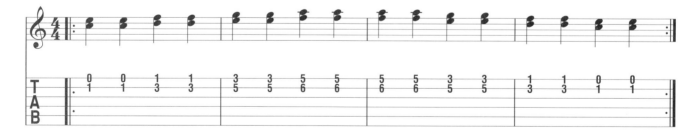

Again, there are no hard and fast rules relating to which fingers to use. In fact, it's a good idea to get used to playing any string with any finger, as certain pieces will require some alternate fingerings.

Now let's try those techniques on "Ode to Joy." (You can use *i–m* or *m–a* throughout.)

ODE TO JOY

Ex. 12

By Ludwig van Beethoven

We can also play two strings at once using the thumb and fingers. It's a little trickier of a technique, as the thumb and fingers move in opposite directions. It should feel a bit like snapping your fingers. Strive to pluck both notes simultaneously. Use the thumb (*p*) to play the lowest note, and use *i* or *m* to play the higher note. Also experiment with alternating *i* and *m*.

Ex. 13

Ex. 14

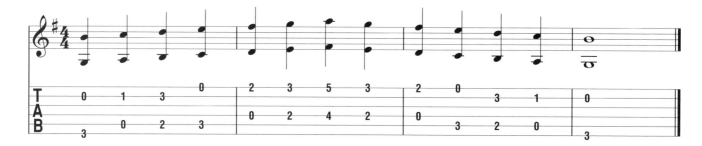

Notice how the left-hand fingering gets trickier now that we need to play changing two-note intervals. In the next examples, we'll take the same progression but now add repeating higher notes as well as repeating bass notes. Again, you can use the same finger for repeating the higher notes as well as trying some alternating fingers.

Ex. 15

Ex. 16

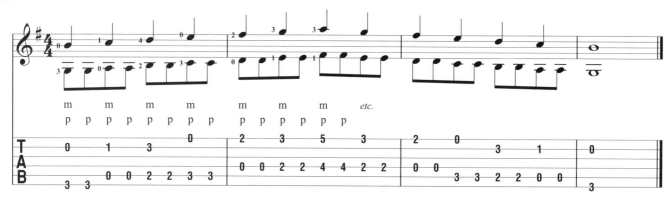

DIVISI NOTATION

When a guitar part has two distinct voices, such as in the two previous examples, we separate them using *divisi* notation. In most cases, the part (or voice) played by the thumb will be down-stemmed, while the other voice (played with the fingers) will be up-stemmed. This also helps show how the bass note might sustain over the higher melody.

MELODY OVER SUSTAINING BASS NOTES

One of the magical elements of fingerpicking is when we can play a melody over a sustained bass note, giving the illusion of two guitars playing at once. This is what draws many players to fingerpicking. With this technique, our solo arrangements will sound full and complete, combining both elements of melody and accompaniment. To start, we'll try a song with open strings as the bass notes. Be sure to let those open strings ring under the melody.

SILENT NIGHT

Ex. 17

Words by Joseph Mohr
Translated by John F. Young
Music by Franz X. Gruber

Let's try another song, this time with a little more movement in the melody.

MINUET

Ex. 18

By Johann Sebastian Bach

The next challenge is to get melody notes to sustain mover a fretted bass note. This takes an extra bit of left-hand dexterity, so let's try an exercise before we jump into a song. Really focus on keeping that fretted bass note down under the changing melody notes. We can deal with the tricky fingering in the second measure two ways: use the first and third fingers on the F and A, and grab the C with your second finger; or use a *hinged barre* technique where you play the F and A with first and second fingers, leaving the barre open to get the second string (B), then come down with the barre to get the C. Both techniques will be demonstrated in the video.

Now we'll try these techniques with a popular Beatles tune. Again, make sure the bass notes ring for their full duration.

LET IT BE

Words and Music by John Lennon and Paul McCartney

RIGHT-HAND SYNCOPATION

All the pieces and exercises so far have had melody notes and bass notes fall on the same beat. That won't always be the case, so we need to develop the ability to play syncopated rhythms with the right hand between the thumb and fingers. First, let's try an exercise that simply alternates between your thumb and fingers.

Ex. 21

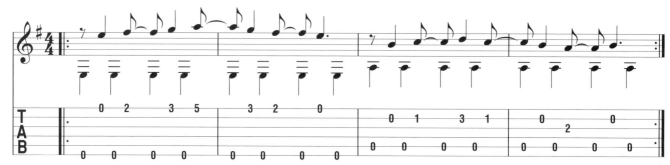

For the next exercise, notice how the second melody note comes in a half beat before the second bass note. If this exercise—or any of the ones to follow—prove too difficult to read, you can listen to the audio/video demonstrations to understand the rhythms and get them in your head.

Ex. 22

To further get the feel for this syncopation, we can add quarter-note rhythms to the bass notes.

Ex. 23

Now let's put some of that syncopation practice to work in a few songs. Again, listen to the recorded audio demo to hear what these rhythms sound like.

Ex. 24

RADIOACTIVE

Words and Music by Daniel Reynolds, Benjamin McKee,
Daniel Sermon, Alexander Grant and Josh Mosser

LET RING

Divisi notation is not always used for fingerstyle guitar arrangements. Oftentimes, a piece will be written in standard "one voice" notation, but it might include an indication to *let ring*. This simply means to hold down any possible chords and let notes ring together as much as possible.

Notice the syncopation here between the melody and bass notes on the verse for "Rolling in the Deep." Keep that thumb pumping steady quarter notes while the melody places some notes in between. Play with a capo on the third fret to be in tune with the original recording.

Ex. 25

ROLLING IN THE DEEP

Words and Music by Adele Adkins and Paul Epworth

"Stay with Me" features some hammer-ons in the verse melody and then some right-hand syncopation in the chorus. Make sure you play those hammer-ons evenly and don't rush. Again, we'll use a capo to be in tune with the original recording, this time on the fifth fret.

Ex. 26

STAY WITH ME

Words and Music by Sam Smith, James Napier,
William Edward Phillips, Tom Petty and Jeff Lynne

Capo V

Verse

let ring throughout

Chorus

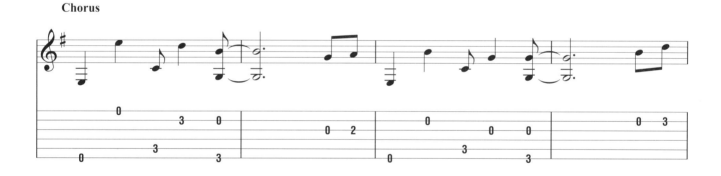

ACCOMPANIMENT PATTERNS

Think of fingerpicking accompaniment patterns as the fingerstyle equivalent of strumming. Typically, we'll take a chord and repeat a pattern, much like we would with a strum pattern. We can use these patterns to accompany the melody (either vocals or instrumental) or simply to spice up a solo arrangement when there is some dead space between melody notes. It's also a great way to build fingerstyle technique, as the repetitive patterns create a perfect practice routine. Let's take a look at some common fingerpicking patterns.

Ex. 27

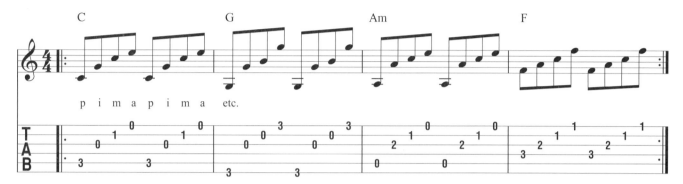

We can take that same progression and just reverse part of the pattern.

Ex. 28

Now let's try mixing things up a little bit with a new progression and pattern.

Ex. 29

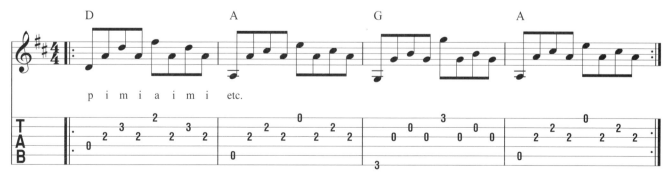

As you can imagine, the variations for fingerpicking patterns are nearly endless. In the next chapter, we'll take a look at *Travis picking*, a new technique that will open up even more possibilities. For now, take a look at the guitar part for the song "Hallelujah," which uses yet another pattern.

Ex. 30

HALLELUJAH
featured in the DreamWorks Motion Picture *SHREK*

Capo V

Words and Music by Leonard Cohen

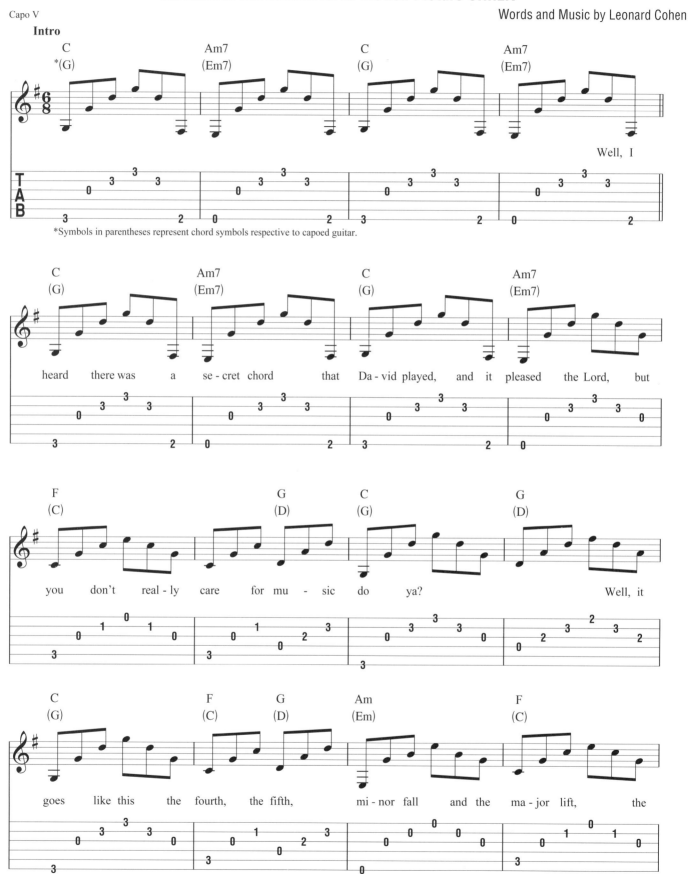

*Symbols in parentheses represent chord symbols respective to capoed guitar.

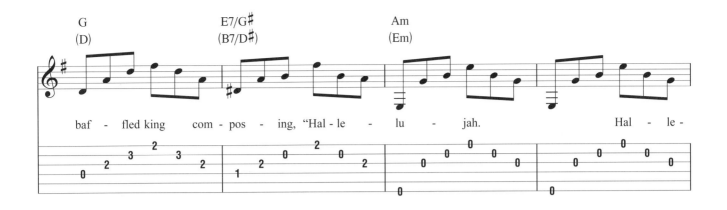

baf - fled king com - pos - ing, "Hal - le - lu - jah. Hal - le -

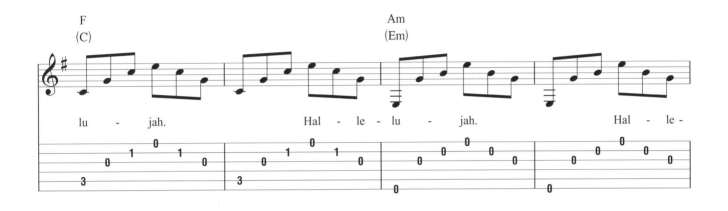

lu - jah. Hal - le - lu - jah. Hal - le -

lu - jah, Hal - le - lu -

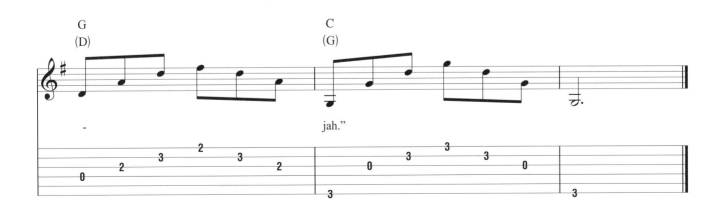

- jah."

In addition to picking single notes, we can also play *block-style* chords by plucking multiple notes. This makes a great accompaniment option. You'll want to use the planting technique that we discussed in Chapter 2, and make sure all the notes are sounding at the same time.

Ex. 31

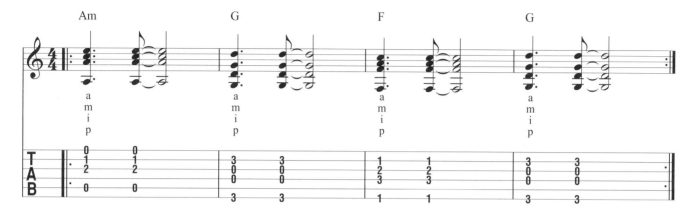

We can further enhance this planting technique by actively hitting the strings in time, creating a popular technique used by fingerstyle guitarists. Keep your fingers in line with the strings you want to pluck, and lightly strike the strings in a planting motion on beats 2 and 4. This will essentially create a rest on those beats, as the notes will stop ringing and the slapping will produce a muted percussive sound. These hits will be notated with Xs in both the notation and the tab. We'll voice the chords a little differently in order to keep the strings we're plucking the same throughout.

Ex. 32

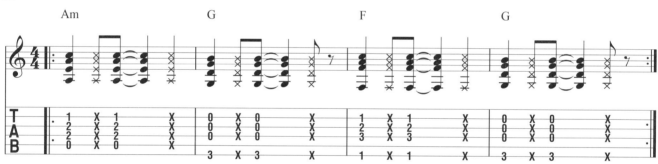

Here's the main guitar riff from the big hit by Ed Sheeran, using this exact technique.

Ex. 33

THINKING OUT LOUD

Words and Music by Ed Sheeran and Amy Wadge

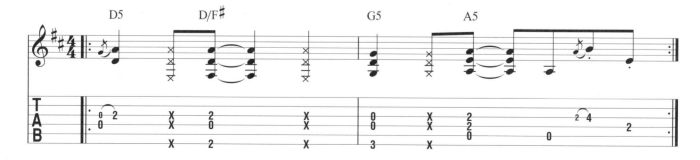

As you progress with your fingerpicking technique, you'll want to be able to pluck block-style chords without the need to plant. Keep your fingers in formation just above the strings. When ready to pluck, move them as a unit. This is the same technique we work on for getting quick chord changes with the left hand; form the chord in the air just above the strings and then come down as a unit. Let's try some repeated block-style chords now in an exercise.

Ex. 34

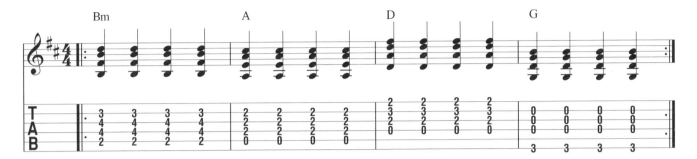

Here are a few popular song intros that use the repeated block-style chords. "Perfect" uses repeated chords, while "Hey There Delilah" alternates the chords with a bass note. "Shallow" combines the use of block chords with some arpeggiation and melody notes.

PERFECT

Words and Music by Ed Sheeran

Ex. 35

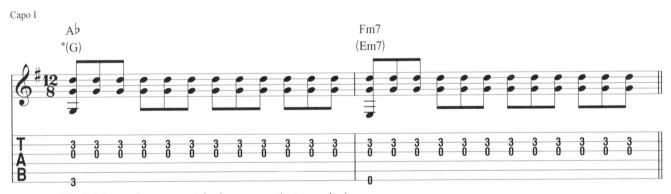

*Symbols in parentheses represent chord names respective to capoed guitar.
Symbols above reflect actual sounding chords. Chord symbols reflect overall harmony.

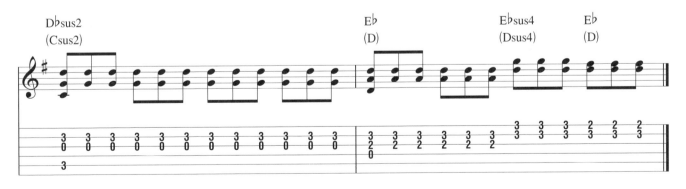

HEY THERE DELILAH

Words and Music by Tom Higgenson

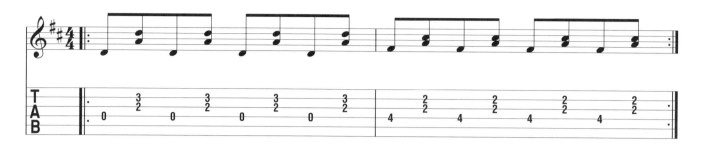

SHALLOW
from *A STAR IS BORN*

Words and Music by Stefani Germanotta, Mark Ronson,
Andrew Wyatt and Anthony Rossomando

TRAVIS PICKING

One of the most popular techniques in fingerstyle guitar is Travis picking. It was named after the country guitar legend Merle Travis and has been used widely by Chet Atkins, Jerry Reed, Tommy Emmanuel, and countless others. Simply put, it's a pattern that involves playing two alternating bass notes with the thumb while the fingers fill in with melody notes. We briefly covered this previously, but here's the most basic Travis pattern on a C chord. Be sure to get that thumb bouncing on the fifth and fourth strings.

Ex. 38

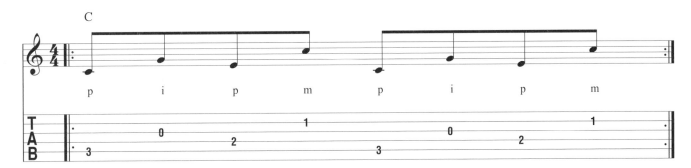

We can try that same idea on a G chord. This time, the thumb will bounce between the sixth and fourth strings.

Ex. 39

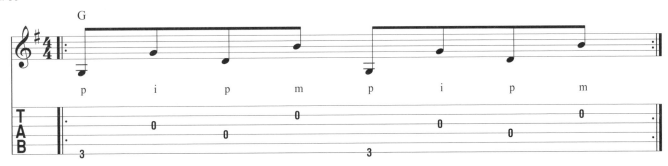

If we're playing a D chord—or any four-string chord, for that matter—the thumb will play strings 4 and 3.

Ex. 40

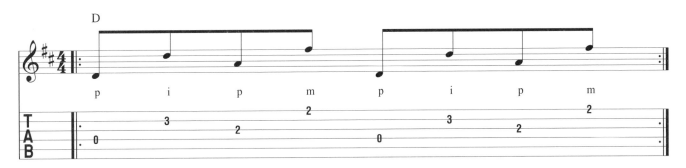

There are many variations on the Travis picking pattern, but the basic concept is always the same: the thumb plays alternate string downbeats while the fingers add melody notes above. In general, the pattern established in the beginning of a song will be used throughout. So if a new song presents an unfamiliar pattern, you'll have many repeats to practice it. Let's try a few new patterns here with some chord changes.

Ex. 41

This one adds the *a* finger.

Ex. 42

We can even add melody notes that play together with the thumb.

Ex. 43

Now let's take a look at a few popular songs that employ Travis picking.

LANDSLIDE

Words and Music by Stevie Nicks

Ex. 44

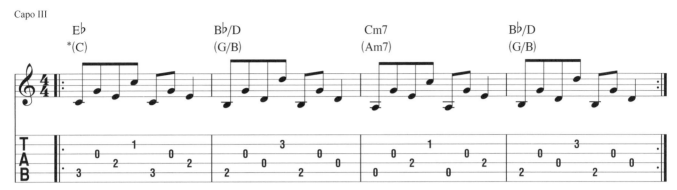

*Symbols in parentheses represent chord names respective to capoed guitar.

The intro for Train's "Marry Me" has a standard Travis pattern, but it also features some trickier left-hand fingering options. For the Fsus2, try either grabbing that low F on the sixth string with your second finger or with your thumb over the neck. Another option would be to play the high C with your second finger and fret the low F with the first.

MARRY ME

Words and Music by David Katz, Pat Monahan and Sam Hollander

Ex. 45

"Blackbird," by the Beatles, makes another great Travis picking study. Although Paul McCartney didn't technically play it in the true Travis style, he employed an interesting first-finger strumming technique on some sections instead. Still, the groove and chords set up nicely for a Travis-picked example. The thumb will take care of the bass note (either fifth or sixth string) and the third string. You can use any finger (or combination of fingers) for the higher notes, but our suggested fingering is to use the *m* finger throughout.

BLACKBIRD

Ex. 46

Words and Music by John Lennon and Paul McCartney

Finally, let's take a look at the intro from one of the most popular Travis-picked tunes, the '70s classic, "Dust in the Wind," from Kansas.

Ex. 47

DUST IN THE WIND

Words and Music by Kerry Livgren

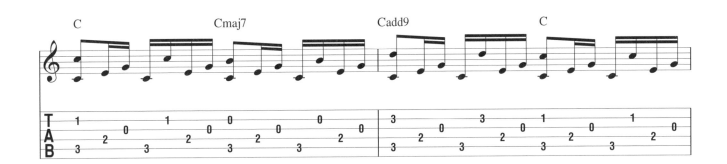

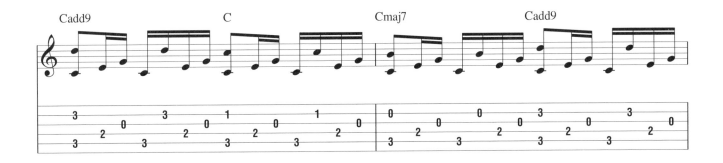

PUTTING IT ALL TOGETHER

The focus of this chapter will be to take all we've learned and use it for some full song arrangements while also adding some finishing touches to our technique. Up to this point, we've either played accompaniment or a simple bass note with melody. Now we'll take our techniques and use them for expanding the harmony in a melody, as well as incorporating some signature riffs within a solo arrangement.

Ex. 48

EVERY BREATH YOU TAKE

Sometimes, you'll find a song that has such an iconic and signature guitar part that it truly defines the song. When that's the case, we must try and include it when doing a fingerstyle arrangement. However, many times we can't just play the riff as it was played, as the key may not work out the best for arranging the melody. In this particular case, we moved the key down a whole step to G. You can also capo it up two frets to match the original recording. We'll play the intro riff and then incorporate it into the verse in between melody notes. To further sound like the original, use *palm muting* on the intro. It does, however, put the right hand at a slightly different angle when fingerpicking, so it might take some getting used to.

Music and Lyrics by Sting

*Symbols in parentheses represent chord names respective to capoed guitar and reflect overall harmony.

AFRICA

Now we'll look at a song that doesn't have an iconic guitar part, but still has an iconic riff. Just because it's not played on guitar doesn't mean we can't arrange it for guitar. The opening riff for Toto's "Africa" is played on a keyboard, but it arranges nicely for guitar if we move it down a whole step. This transposition also makes the rest of the song a bit more playable on guitar. In general, when arranging for guitar, we try to utilize open strings whenever possible, as well as avoiding too many uncomfortable barre chords. The more strings we can have ringing, the fuller the arrangement will sound. In the case of moving a song to a lower key, we can simply capo it up if we want to match the original.

There are some rests to be aware of in the opening riff. Since they're open notes, we'll need to mute with our right-hand fingers. Utilize the planting technique that we discussed in Chapter 2. There's also some challenging syncopation between the melody and accompaniment during the chorus. Also note the suggested left-hand fingerings. In an effort to allow melody notes to ring, oftentimes we need to look ahead to the next measure and choose a fingering that will work for both measures.

Words and Music by David Paich and Jeff Porcaro

*Symbols in parentheses represent chord names respective to capoed guitar and reflect general harmony

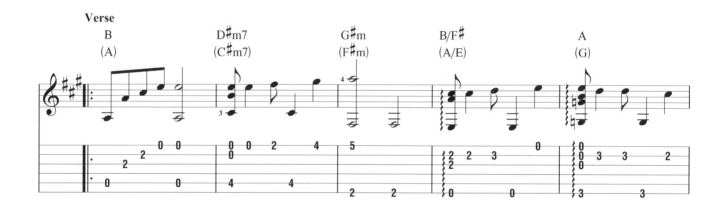

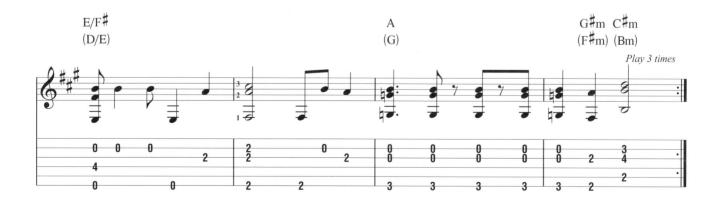

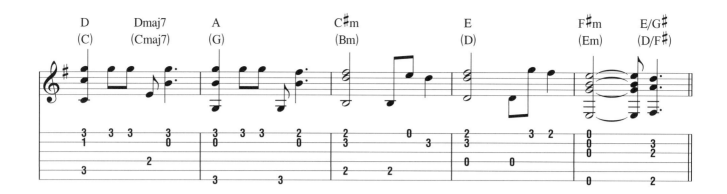

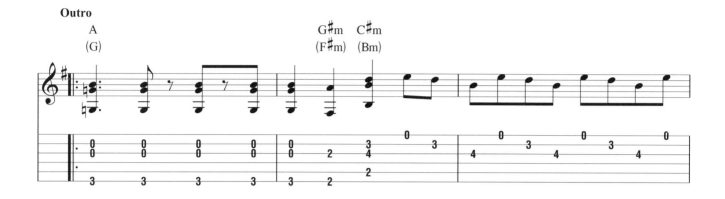

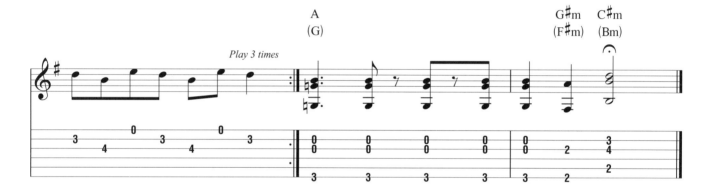

Ex. 50

FREIGHT TRAIN

When we worked on Travis picking in Chapter 5, we used it exclusively for accompaniment. However, Travis picking can also be used in combination with a melody, creating a challenging solo arrangement. Now, not every song lends itself well to a Travis pattern, but the original version of "Freight Train" has Elizabeth Cotten playing a Travis pattern along with melody for the intro before continuing with a Travis pattern while she sings. Solo arrangements of "Freight Train" have become standard fare for any serious fingerstyle guitarist, with great versions recorded by many of the fingerpicking masters. Interesting note: Elizabeth Cotten was a self-taught, left-handed guitarist who played a guitar strung for a right-handed player, but she played it upside down. This position meant that she would play the bass lines with her fingers and the melody with her thumb. Do not try this at home!

We'll stick to the open position for our version of "Freight Train." There aren't any tricky fingerings, so you can really concentrate on getting that melody to pop out while the Travis pattern rolls along. If you feel comfortable with the technique, try fretting the low F in measures 11–12 with your thumb over the neck. This is a popular technique with fingerstyle playing, as it frees up the fingers to play melody. It takes a while to get used to, and having a long thumb really helps. However, even with a normal sized hand, with a bit of practice, this technique will settle in and become a useful option. On the first and second endings, we're playing a C with an alternate bass, making it a three-note Travis bass pattern instead of just two. This is another popular technique in Travis picking. In this case, you can either fret an entire C/G with four fingers, or simply move the third finger from the fifth to the sixth string.

Words and Music by Elizabeth Cotten

*Chord symbols reflect overall harmony.

IN MY LIFE

Ex. 51

We conclude with this Beatles classic. Here, we've changed the key to make the signature riff and melody easier to play in the open position. It has some hints of Travis picking in the intro, filling in between the main riff. Once we get to the verse, we're playing melody over bass notes, and that treatment continues on through the chorus. You'll find a couple of awkward fingerings when fretting bass notes on the first fret, so pay attention to the suggested fingerings.

Words and Music by John Lennon and Paul McCartney

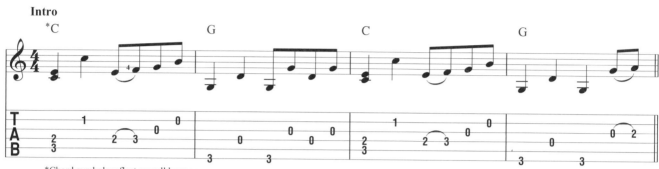

*Chord symbols reflect overall harmony.

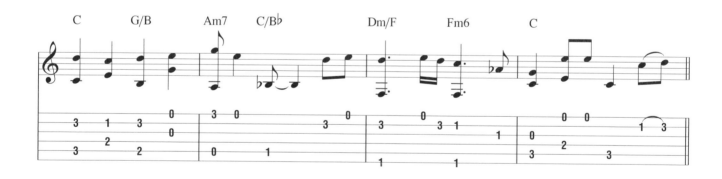

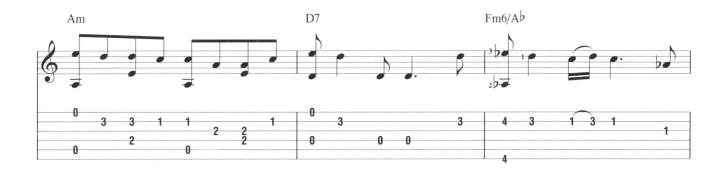

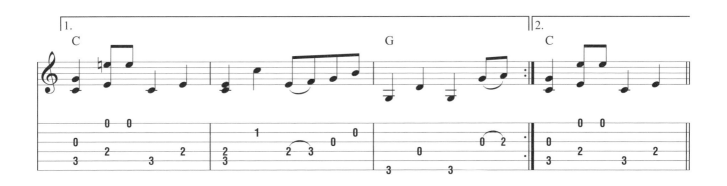

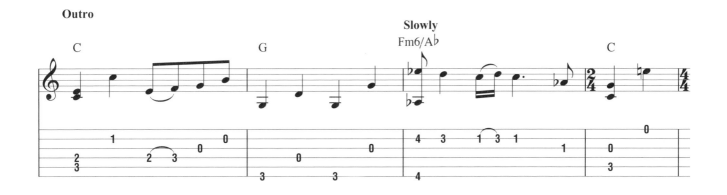

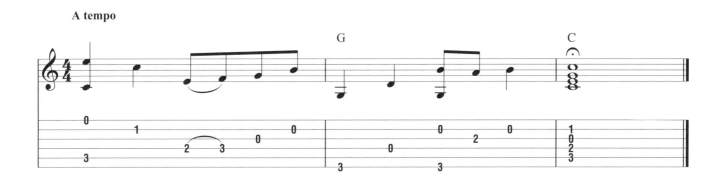

GUITAR NOTATION LEGEND

Guitar music can be notated three different ways: on a *musical staff*, in *tablature*, and in *rhythm slashes*.

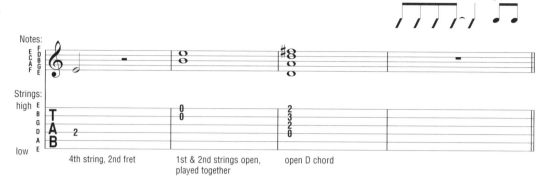

RHYTHM SLASHES are written above the staff. Strum chords in the rhythm indicated. Use the chord diagrams found at the top of the first page of the transcription for the appropriate chord voicings. Round noteheads indicate single notes.

THE MUSICAL STAFF shows pitches and rhythms and is divided by bar lines into measures. Pitches are named after the first seven letters of the alphabet.

TABLATURE graphically represents the guitar fingerboard. Each horizontal line represents a string, and each number represents a fret.

4th string, 2nd fret   1st & 2nd strings open, played together   open D chord

---

HALF-STEP BEND: Strike the note and bend up 1/2 step.

BEND AND RELEASE: Strike the note and bend up as indicated, then release back to the original note. Only the first note is struck.

HAMMER-ON: Strike the first (lower) note with one finger, then sound the higher note (on the same string) with another finger by fretting it without picking.

TRILL: Very rapidly alternate between the notes indicated by continuously hammering on and pulling off.

PICK SCRAPE: The edge of the pick is rubbed down (or up) the string, producing a scratchy sound.

TREMOLO PICKING: The note is picked as rapidly and continuously as possible.

WHOLE-STEP BEND: Strike the note and bend up one step.

PRE-BEND: Bend the note as indicated, then strike it.

PULL-OFF: Place both fingers on the notes to be sounded. Strike the first note and without picking, pull the finger off to sound the second (lower) note.

TAPPING: Hammer ("tap") the fret indicated with the pick-hand index or middle finger and pull off to the note fretted by the fret hand.

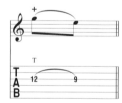

MUFFLED STRINGS: A percussive sound is produced by laying the fret hand across the string(s) without depressing, and striking them with the pick hand.

VIBRATO BAR DIVE AND RETURN: The pitch of the note or chord is dropped a specified number of steps (in rhythm), then returned to the original pitch.

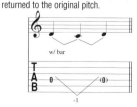

GRACE NOTE BEND: Strike the note and immediately bend up as indicated.

VIBRATO: The string is vibrated by rapidly bending and releasing the note with the fretting hand.

LEGATO SLIDE: Strike the first note and then slide the same fret-hand finger up or down to the second note. The second note is not struck.

NATURAL HARMONIC: Strike the note while the fret-hand lightly touches the string directly over the fret indicated.

PALM MUTING: The note is partially muted by the pick hand lightly touching the string(s) just before the bridge.

VIBRATO BAR SCOOP: Depress the bar just before striking the note, then quickly release the bar.

SLIGHT (MICROTONE) BEND: Strike the note and bend up 1/4 step.

WIDE VIBRATO: The pitch is varied to a greater degree by vibrating with the fretting hand.

SHIFT SLIDE: Same as legato slide, except the second note is struck.

PINCH HARMONIC: The note is fretted normally and a harmonic is produced by adding the edge of the thumb or the tip of the index finger of the pick hand to the normal pick attack.

RAKE: Drag the pick across the strings indicated with a single motion.

VIBRATO BAR DIP: Strike the note and then immediately drop a specified number of steps, then release back to the original pitch.

HAL LEONARD GUITAR METHOD

METHOD BOOKS, SONGBOOKS AND REFERENCE BOOKS

THE HAL LEONARD GUITAR METHOD is designed for anyone just learning to play acoustic or electric guitar. It is based on years of teaching guitar students of all ages, and it also reflects some of the best guitar teaching ideas from around the world. This comprehensive method includes:

A learning sequence carefully paced with clear instructions; popular songs which increase the incentive to learn to play; versatility – can be used as self-instruction or with a teacher; audio accompaniments so that students have fun and sound great while practicing.

BOOK 1
00699010 Book Only
00699027 Book/Online Audio
00697341 Book/Online Audio + DVD
00697318 DVD Only
00155480 Deluxe Beginner Edition
          (Book, CD, DVD, Online Audio/
          Video & Chord Poster)

COMPLETE (BOOKS 1, 2 & 3)
00699040 Book Only
00697342 Book/Online Audio

BOOK 2
00699020 Book Only
00697313 Book/Online Audio

BOOK 3
00699030 Book Only
00697316 Book/Online Audio

Prices, contents and availability subject to change without notice.

STYLISTIC METHODS

ACOUSTIC GUITAR
00697347 Method Book/Online Audio
00237969 Songbook/Online Audio

BLUEGRASS GUITAR
00697405 Method Book/Online Audio

BLUES GUITAR
00697326 Method Book/Online Audio (9" x 12")
00697344 Method Book/Online Audio (6" x 9")
00697385 Songbook/Online Audio (9" x 12")
00248636 Kids Method Book/Online Audio

BRAZILIAN GUITAR
00697415 Method Book/Online Audio

CHRISTIAN GUITAR
00695947 Method Book/Online Audio

CLASSICAL GUITAR
00697376 Method Book/Online Audio

COUNTRY GUITAR
00697337 Method Book/Online Audio
00354721 Songbook/Online Audio

FINGERSTYLE GUITAR
00697378 Method Book/Online Audio
00697432 Songbook/Online Audio

FLAMENCO GUITAR
00697363 Method Book/Online Audio

FOLK GUITAR
00697414 Method Book/Online Audio

JAZZ GUITAR
00695359 Book/Online Audio
00697386 Songbook/Online Audio

JAZZ-ROCK FUSION
00697387 Book/Online Audio

R&B GUITAR
00697356 Book/Online Audio
00697433 Songbook/CD Pack

ROCK GUITAR
00697319 Book/Online Audio
00697383 Songbook/Online Audio

ROCKABILLY GUITAR
00697407 Book/Online Audio

OTHER METHOD BOOKS

BARITONE GUITAR METHOD
00242055 Book/Online Audio

GUITAR FOR KIDS
00865003 Method Book 1/Online Audio
00697402 Songbook/Online Audio
00128437 Method Book 2/Online Audio

MUSIC THEORY FOR GUITARISTS
00695790 Book/Online Audio

PEDAL STEEL GUITAR METHOD
00695857 Book/Online Audio

TENOR GUITAR METHOD
00148330 Book/Online Audio

12-STRING GUITAR METHOD
00249528 Book/Online Audio

METHOD SUPPLEMENTS

ARPEGGIO FINDER
00697352 6" x 9" Edition
00697351 9" x 12" Edition

BARRE CHORDS
00697406 Book/Online Audio

CHORD, SCALE & ARPEGGIO FINDER
00697410 Book Only

GUITAR TECHNIQUES
00697389 Book/Online Audio

INCREDIBLE CHORD FINDER
00697200 6" x 9" Edition
00697208 9" x 12" Edition

INCREDIBLE SCALE FINDER
00695568 6" x 9" Edition
00695490 9" x 12" Edition

LEAD LICKS
00697345 Book/Online Audio

RHYTHM RIFFS
00697346 Book/Online Audio

SONGBOOKS

CLASSICAL GUITAR PIECES
00697388 Book/Online Audio

EASY POP MELODIES
00697281 Book Only
00697440 Book/Online Audio

(MORE) EASY POP MELODIES
00697280 Book Only
00697269 Book/Online Audio

(EVEN MORE) EASY POP MELODIES
00699154 Book Only
00697439 Book/Online Audio

EASY POP RHYTHMS
00697336 Book Only
00697441 Book/Online Audio

(MORE) EASY POP RHYTHMS
00697338 Book Only
00697322 Book/Online Audio

(EVEN MORE) EASY POP RHYTHMS
00697340 Book Only
00697323 Book/Online Audio

EASY POP CHRISTMAS MELODIES
00697417 Book Only
00697416 Book/Online Audio

EASY POP CHRISTMAS RHYTHMS
00278177 Book Only
00278175 Book/Online Audio

EASY SOLO GUITAR PIECES
00110407 Book Only

REFERENCE

GUITAR PRACTICE PLANNER
00697401 Book Only

GUITAR SETUP & MAINTENANCE
00697427 6" x 9" Edition
00697421 9" x 12" Edition

For more info, songlists, or to purchase these and more books from your favorite music retailer, go to

halleonard.com

HAL•LEONARD®

FINGERPICKING GUITAR BOOKS

Hone your fingerpicking skills with these great songbooks featuring solo guitar arrangements in standard notation and tablature. The arrangements in these books are carefully written for intermediate-level guitarists. Each song combines melody and harmony in one superb guitar fingerpicking arrangement. Each book also includes an introduction to basic fingerstyle guitar.

 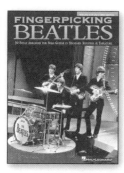    

Fingerpicking Acoustic
00699614 15 songs......................$15.99

Fingerpicking Acoustic Classics
00160211 15 songs......................$16.99

Fingerpicking Acoustic Hits
00160202 15 songs......................$15.99

Fingerpicking Acoustic Rock
00699764 14 songs......................$17.99

Fingerpicking Ballads
00699717 15 songs......................$15.99

Fingerpicking Beatles
00699049 30 songs......................$24.99

Fingerpicking Beethoven
00702390 15 pieces......................$10.99

Fingerpicking Blues
00701277 15 songs......................$12.99

Fingerpicking Broadway Favorites
00699843 15 songs......................$9.99

Fingerpicking Campfire
00275964 15 songs......................$14.99

Fingerpicking Celtic Folk
00701148 15 songs......................$12.99

Fingerpicking Children's Songs
00699712 15 songs......................$9.99

Fingerpicking Christian
00701076 15 songs......................$12.99

Fingerpicking Christmas
00699599 20 carols......................$12.99

Fingerpicking Christmas Songs
00171333 15 songs......................$10.99

Fingerpicking Classical
00699620 15 pieces......................$14.99

Fingerpicking Country
00699687 17 songs......................$14.99

Fingerpicking Disney
00699711 15 songs......................$17.99

Fingerpicking Early Jazz Standards
00276565 15 songs......................$14.99

Fingerpicking Duke Ellington
00699845 15 songs......................$9.99

Fingerpicking Enya
00701161 15 songs......................$17.99

Fingerpicking Film Score Music
00160143 15 songs......................$15.99

Fingerpicking Gospel
00701059 15 songs......................$12.99

Fingerpicking Hit Songs
00160195 15 songs......................$15.99

Fingerpicking Hymns
00699688 15 hymns......................$14.99

Fingerpicking Irish Songs
00701965 15 songs......................$12.99

Fingerpicking Italian Songs
00159778 15 songs......................$12.99

Fingerpicking Jazz Favorites
00699844 15 songs......................$15.99

Fingerpicking Jazz Standards
00699840 15 songs......................$12.99

Fingerpicking Elton John
00237495 15 songs......................$17.99

Fingerpicking Latin Standards
00699837 15 songs......................$17.99

Fingerpicking Love Songs
00699841 15 songs......................$16.99

Fingerpicking Love Standards
00699836 15 songs......................$9.99

Fingerpicking Lullabyes
00701276 16 songs......................$9.99

Fingerpicking Movie Music
00699919 15 songs......................$14.99

Fingerpicking Mozart
00699794 15 pieces......................$10.99

Fingerpicking Pop
00699615 15 songs......................$16.99

Fingerpicking Popular Hits
00139079 14 songs......................$12.99

Fingerpicking Praise
00699714 15 songs......................$16.99

Fingerpicking Rock
00699716 15 songs......................$15.99

Fingerpicking Standards
00699613 17 songs......................$15.99

Fingerpicking Worship
00700554 15 songs......................$15.99

Fingerpicking Neil Young – Greatest Hits
00700134 16 songs......................$17.99

Fingerpicking Yuletide
00699654 16 songs......................$12.99

HAL•LEONARD®

Order these and more great publications from your favorite music retailer at
halleonard.com

Prices, contents and availability subject to change without notice.